The glen

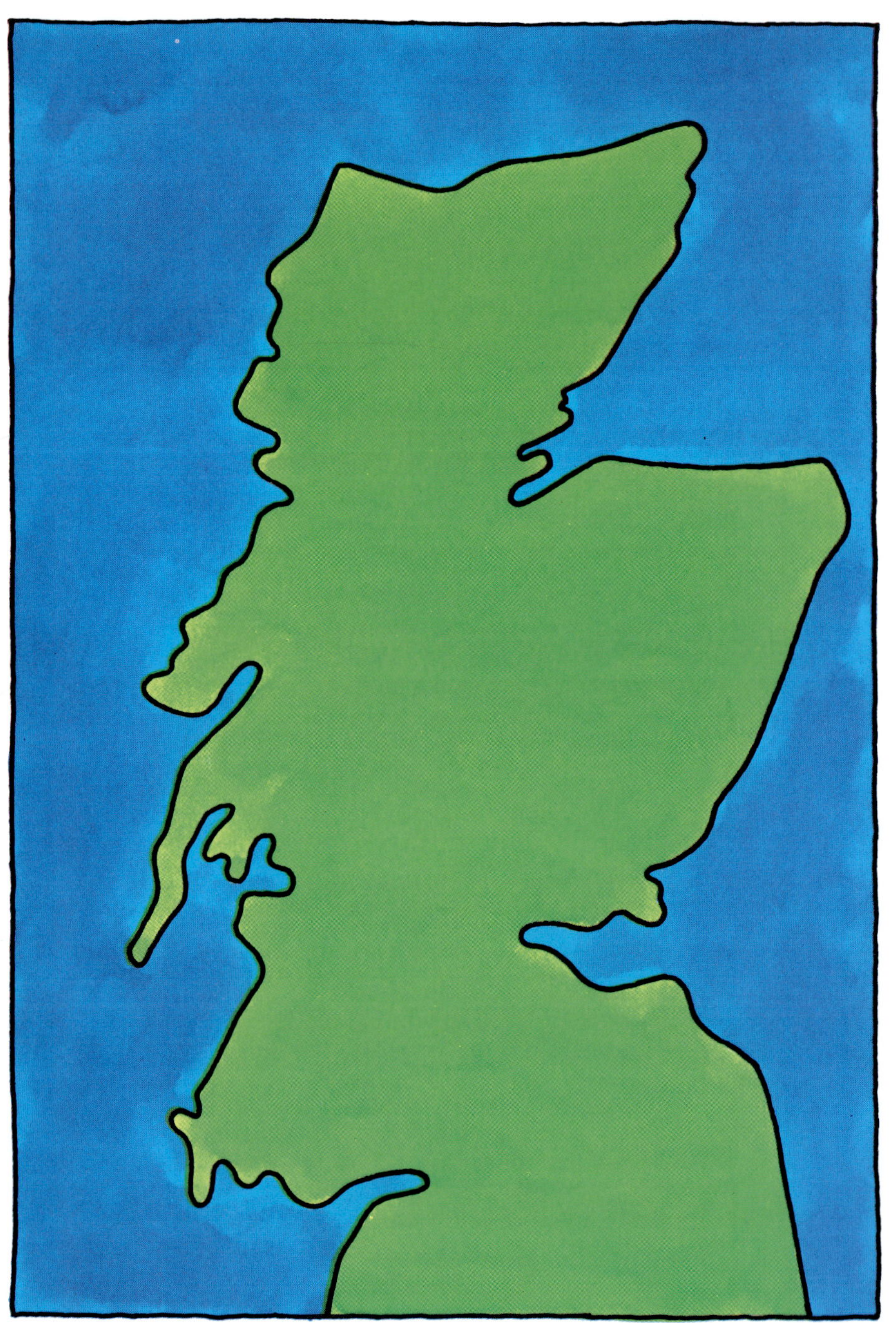

This is Scotland.

In Scotland there is a glen.
This is the glen.
This glen is called the glen Macfuzz.

Draw the glen and colour it in.
Write
This is the glen Macfuzz.
The glen Macfuzz is in Scotland.

There are some big green hills
next to the glen Macfuzz.

Can you see the yellow sun?

The sun is coming up from these hills.

There are some trees on the hills.

The trees are green and brown.

Draw and colour the green hills.

Draw the trees.

**Draw the sun coming up and
colour it yellow.**

Write

The sun comes up from the green hills.

There is a blue river coming down
from the green hills.

This river is little at first.

The little blue river creeps in and out
of the trees and down to a rock.

There is a big crack in this rock.

The little blue river drops down
from this crack.

Write

The river comes down from the hills.

Draw this.

The little blue river comes down
into the glen Macfuzz.
This river is called the river Mac.
Can you see some trees next to
the river Mac?
There are some crofts under these
trees.

Macfuzz
the buzz

This is a croft.

This croft is yellow and brown.

Can you see some trees at the back
of the croft?

Can you see the letter box?

Can you read the words
on the letter box?

Draw the croft and colour it in.

Draw the letter box.

Write the words on it.

M

In the little yellow and brown croft
there lives a fuzzbuzz.

He is called Macfuzz the buzz.

This is Macfuzz the buzz.

Draw Macfuzz the buzz.

Write

This is Macfuzz the buzz.

He lives in a little croft in Scotland.

There are some more yellow and
brown crofts next to the river Mac.
There are some more fuzzbuzzes
in these crofts.
Can you see them?

The fuzzbuzzes come out to see
Macfuzz the buzz.

He is the chief of these fuzzbuzzes.

In Scotland these fuzzbuzzes
are called a clan.

This clan is called the clan Macfuzz.

The clan Macfuzz lives in
the glen Macfuzz.

Macfuzz the buzz is the chief
of the clan.

Draw some of the clan.

Write

Macfuzz the buzz is the chief
of this clan.

Big Ben

Macfuzz and the clan love the glen.

They love the little yellow and brown crofts.

They love the blue river Mac.

They love the green trees.

They love to go up into the green hills.

Draw them going up into the hills.

Write

They love to go up into the hills.

Macfuzz and his clan are up
in the hills now.

They can see down into the glen
Macfuzz.

They can see the river Mac coming
out of the trees.

They can see it going down the glen.

They can see the little crofts under
the green trees.

They are happy to see these things.

The little fuzzbuzzes from the clan
come out into the glen.

They come out to play.

They love to get up into the trees
next to the crofts.

This is good fun.

Draw the fuzzbuzzes in the trees.

Write

The little fuzzbuzzes love to play.

The little fuzzbuzzes go down
to the river to play.
They love to play under the trees
next to the river.
They love to jump into the river.
This is good fun.
They are happy.

Can you see some more fuzzbuzzes
down at the river?

Can you see a little fuzzbuzz
with a red ribbon and an apple?

Can you see a fuzzbuzz in a tree?

Can you see a fuzzbuzz jumping onto
a rock?

Can you see a fuzzbuzz with a van?

Can you see a fuzzbuzz with
a black umbrella?

Can you see a fuzzbuzz going down
the river in a tin box?

**Draw some of the things
these fuzzbuzzes play with.**

The clan come back down
from the green hills now.
The little fuzzbuzzes come back
from the river.
In the end, they go into the little
crofts under the trees.

Write
The clan go back into the little crofts.

In the glen Macfuzz the sun goes down.

The sun is big and red now.
The clan are going to sleep.